THE POET'S
TOOLBOX

The Free and the Brave

A Collection of Poems About the United States

Compiled and Annotated
by Patricia M. Stockland

Illustrated by
Sara Rojo Pérez

Compass Point Books
151 Good Counsel Drive
P.O. Box 669
Mankato, MN 56002-0669

Permissions and Acknowledgements: Statue of Liberty inscription, 6. Public domain. "The Dream Keeper,"
7. From THE COLLECTED POEMS OF LANGSTON HUGHES by Langston Hughes, copyright © 1994 by The Estate
of Langston Hughes. Used by permission of Alfred A. Knopf, a division of Random House, Inc. "Buffalo Dusk,"
8. "Buffalo Dusk" from SMOKE AND STEEL by Carl Sandburg, copyright 1920 by Harcourt, Inc. and renewed
1948 by Carl Sandburg, reprinted by permission of the publisher. "steam engines," 9. "Steam Engines" from
PEACOCK AND OTHER POEMS by Valerie Worth. Copyright © 2000 by Valerie Worth. Reprinted by permission
of Farrar, Straus and Giroux, LLC. "The Pioneer," 10. Every effort has been made to contact the author.
Compass Point Books does not take credit for the authorship, ownership, or copyright of this poem. "Until We
Built a Cabin," 11. From THAT'S WHY by Aileen Fisher. Copyright © 1946, 1974 Aileen Fisher. Used by permission
of Marian Reiner on behalf of the Boulder Public Library Foundation. "Grandpa's Trees," 12. By permission of
the author, who controls all rights. "Prayer for Earth," 13. From THE BIG BOOK FOR OUR PLANET, a Dutton
Children's book. Copyright © 1993 by Myra Cohn Livingston. Also included in Livingston collection, FLIGHTS
OF FANCY, A Margaret K. Mc Elderry Book. Used by permission of Marian Reiner. "Aunt Sue's Stories," 14.
From THE COLLECTED POEMS OF LANGSTON HUGHES by Langston Hughes, copyright © 1994 by The Estate of
Langston Hughes. Used by permission of Alfred A. Knopf, a division of Random House, Inc. "When I Grow
Up," 16. Reprinted with the permission of Margaret K. McElderry books, an imprint of Simon & Schuster
Children's Publishing Division from A SUITCASE OF SEAWEED AND OTHER POEMS by Janet S. Wong. Copyright
© 1996 Janet S. Wong. "Poor," 17. From THE WAY THINGS ARE AND OTHER POEMS by Myra Cohn Livingston.
Copyright © 1974 by Myra Cohn Livingston. Used by permission of Marian Reiner. "Commitment in a City,"
18. Reprinted by permission of the author. "City Blockades," 19. Copyright © 1972 by Lee Bennett Hopkins.
First appeared in Charlie's World, published by Bobbs Merrill. Reprinted by permissions of Curtis Brown, Ltd.
"Brooklyn Bridge," 20. "Brooklyn Bridge" from LAUGHING TIME: COLLECTED NONSENSE by William Jay Smith.
Copyright © 1990 by William Jay Smith. Reprinted by permission of Farrar, Straus and Giroux, LLC. "Time to
Play," 21. By permission of author. From Pass It On: African-American Poetry for Children, selected by Wade
Hudson, Scholastic, Inc., 1993. "After the Picnic," 22. Every effort has been made to contact the author.
Compass Point Books does not take credit for the authorship, ownership, or copyright of this poem. "Fourth
of July Night," 23. "Fourth of July Night," from HOP, SKIP AND JUMP! by Dorothy Aldis, copyright 1934,
renewed © 1961 by Dorothy Aldis. Used by permission of G.P. Putnam's Sons, an imprint of Penguin Putnam
Books for Young Readers, a division of Penguin Putnam, Inc. All rights reserved. "Our Flag," 24. From AROUND
THE YEAR by Aileen Fisher. Copyright © 1967, 1995 Aileen Fisher. Used by permission of Marian Reiner for the
Boulder Public Library Foundation. "The Star-Spangled Banner," 25. Public domain.

Content Advisers: Jane K. Volkman, Patricia Kirkpatrick, Ph.D.
Rights Researcher: Nancy Loewen
Designer: The Design Lab

Library of Congress Cataloging-in-Publication Data
The free and the brave : a collection of poems about the United States / compiled and annotated
by Patricia M. Stockland.
   p. cm. — (The poet's toolbox)
Summary: An anthology of poems about the United States, plus "Toolbox tips" that help the reader
understand poetry and how poems are written.
ISBN 978-0-7565-0563-9 (hardcover)
1. United States—Juvenile poetry. 2. Poetry—Authorship—Juvenile literature. 3. Children's poetry,
American. (1. United States—Poetry. 2. American poetry.) I. Stockland, Patricia M. II. Title. III. Series.
PS595.U5F74 2004
808.81'93273—dc22   2003017104

Visit Compass Point Books on the Internet at www.compasspointbooks.com
or e-mail your request to custserv@compasspointbooks.com

A special thank you to John,
Elizabeth, and Chaneen

Table of Contents

NOTE: In this book, words that are defined in the glossary are in **bold** the first time they appear in the text.

Open Your Toolbox

The United States is a large and diverse country. It has hundreds of different areas, people, cultures, and traditions. People have been coming here for freedom for more than 400 years. Maybe you were born and raised in the United States, or maybe you came to the United States from a different nation and culture. Each person experiences the country in a unique way. How do you describe those moments—when you suddenly discover a new tradition, or you hear a part of history that makes you proud, or you go on a trip and find a great part of the country you've never seen before? Poetry can be a way to tell about those things— cities, farms, people, jobs, history, traditions, the flag . . . anything!

WHAT DOES POETRY DO?

Poetry helps energize your imagination. Poetry plays with words in ways you never imagined. Ordinary words are suddenly mysterious or exciting. Poetry opens your ears to different sounds—sentences can play like music. Everyone has smart ideas, and poetry can be a new language with which to share those ideas.

DOES A POET USE A TOOLBOX?

Poets use many different tools and materials to build their poems. Material poets use can be stuff that happens to them every day in their lives. Poets' tools are parts of speech (such as nouns, verbs, and adjectives), ways of writing (like different forms or types of poetry), and the interesting sounds that letters and words make when they're combined (like rhymes and repeated letters). This book will show you some different tools poets use to create poems, and it might even teach you to write some poetry.

HOW DOES THE POET'S TOOLBOX WORK?

First, read all the poems—each one shows you something different about the United States, its history, culture, and people. After you read each one, take a look at the Toolbox Tip on the bottom of the page. These Toolbox Tips will help you understand a poetry tool the writer has used, or they might give you a hint about where the poet found the idea for that poem. Near the back of the book, you'll have the chance to begin using these tools yourself!

The New Colossus: Statue of Liberty Inscription

Give me your tired, your poor,
your huddled masses yearning to breathe free,
the wretched refuse of your teeming shore.
Send these, the homeless, tempest-tossed to me.
I lift my lamp beside the golden door.

—Emma Lazarus

HOPE

People often see the United States as a land of hope and freedom. In this poem, the golden door is a **metaphor** for ideas like hope and freedom. Metaphors, which give the qualities of one thing to another, can help explain such ideas.

The Dream Keeper

Bring me all of your dreams,
You dreamers,
Bring me all of your
Heart melodies
That I may wrap them
In a blue cloud-cloth
Away from the too-rough fingers
Of the world.

—Langston Hughes

Make believe

MAKE BELIEVE
TOOLBOX TIP
Langston Hughes, a famous African-American poet, wrote this poem. He also uses metaphors. The world doesn't really have rough fingers. It could mean that the world is a rough place and the dream keeper can offer protection from it.

7

The Pioneer

He could not breathe in a crowded place—
He wanted his air and his open space.
He watched while civilization neared
On the path through the wilderness Boone had cleared,
Saw highways hiding the Indian trails.
West fled the bear and the elk and the deer—
"I've got to go," said the Pioneer.
He whistled to his dog and called to his wife,
Loaded his rifle and sharpened his knife,
Tossed in his wagon a pan or two—
Texas-bound, to a land plumb new.
They watched him go, and shook each head—
"Shiftless fool—better stay," they said.
Not a sign they saw that might denote
That a Nation rode in his coonskin coat.

—William B. Ruggles

Rhymes for the road

TOOLBOX TIP **RHYMES FOR THE ROAD**
When words end in the same sound, they
rhyme. How many pairs of rhymes can
you find at the ends of these lines?

Until We Built a Cabin

When we lived in a city
(three flights up and down)
I never dreamed how many stars
could show above a town.

When we moved to a village
where lighted streets were few,
I thought I could see ALL the stars,
but, oh, I never knew—

Until we built a cabin
where hills are high and far,
I never knew how many
        many
        stars there really are!

—Aileen Fisher

STANZAS

A blank space divides ideas into **stanzas,** which are like paragraphs for poetry. The poet begins a new thought after skipping a line. This poet also uses stanzas to show different periods of time.

TOOLBOX TIP

Buffalo Dusk

The buffaloes are gone.
And those who saw the buffaloes are gone.
Those who saw the buffaloes by thousands and
    how they pawed the prairie sod into dust
    with their hoofs, their great heads down
    pawing on in a great pageant of dusk,
Those who saw the buffaloes are gone.
And the buffaloes are gone.

—Carl Sandburg

SAY IT AGAIN . . .

TOOLBOX TIP

When the poet repeats the phrase "the buffaloes are gone," he is using **repetition.** This is a good way to make a point, or get a reader to remember something. It also creates the feeling of an echo.

steam engines

They are gone,
All herded into
Scrapyards, the

Grim iron
Locomotives with
Their long boilers,

Their complicated
Plates and domes
And pistons;

But I still
Meet their looming
Ghosts in dreams.

—Valerie Worth

A herd of . . . steam engines?

TOOLBOX TIP

A HERD OF . . . STEAM ENGINES?

This poem sounds like someone is just talking. It's a **free verse** poem—it doesn't use rhyming words or stick to set patterns. Instead, the poet uses other tools to build the poem, such as stanzas and the metaphor of "herded."

Grandpa's Trees

My grandpa built a farmhouse
Half a century ago.
On Arbor Day he planted trees
In one long tidy row.

He says they looked like beanpoles,
So leafless, frail, and small.
He tended them those early years
Though they gave no shade at all.

Today I counted forty trees
Tall-grown and sturdy-stout.
Their branches hug each other
As the wind blows them about.

They've sheltered Grandpa's farmhouse
In every sort of weather.
To me, they're friendly giants
Holding earth and sky together.

—Barbara M. Hales

SAME TREES, DIFFERENT STORY
Comparing and contrasting shows what is the same and different about two or more things, or how something used to be versus what it is like now. It's a great tool to show change. What are some of the differences between the "new" trees and the "old" trees?

TOOLBOX TIP

12

Prayer for Earth

Last night
an owl
called from the hill.
Coyotes howled.
A deer stood still
nibbling at bushes far away.
The moon shone silver.
Let this stay.

Today
two noisy crows
flew by,
their shadows pasted to the sky.
The sun broke out
through clouds of gray.
An iris opened.
Let this stay.

—Myra Cohn Livingston

Can you hear it?

TOOLBOX TIP

CAN YOU HEAR IT?

Poems can perk up more than just your imagination—they can perk up your ears, too. This poet mentions a lot of different sounds. How many animals can you "hear" in the poem?

Aunt Sue's Stories

Aunt Sue has a head full of stories.
Aunt Sue has a whole heart full of stories.
Summer nights on the front porch
Aunt Sue cuddles a brown-faced child to her bosom
And tells him stories.

Black slaves
Working in the hot sun,
And black slaves
Walking in the dewy night,
And black slaves
Singing sorrow songs on the banks of a mighty river
Mingle themselves softly
In the flow of old Aunt Sue's voice,
Mingle themselves softly
In the dark shadows that cross and recross
Aunt Sue's stories.

And the dark-faced child, listening,
Knows that Aunt Sue's stories are real stories.
He knows that Aunt Sue
Never got her stories out of any book at all,
But that they came
Right out of her own life.

And the dark-faced child is quiet
Of a summer night
Listening to Aunt Sue's stories.

—Langston Hughes

Can you see it?

CAN YOU SEE IT?

A poet can really draw a picture for you. This picture in your mind is **imagery.** When you think of Aunt Sue telling her stories, what do you see? Details like "hot sun" and "dewy night" helped create that imagery!

When I Grow Up

I want to be an artist, Grandpa—
write and paint, dance and sing.

    Be accountant.
    Be lawyer.
    Make good living,
    buy good food.
    Back in China,
    in the old days,
    everybody
    so, so poor.
    Eat one chicken,
    work all year.

Grandpa, things are different
here.

—Janet S. Wong

Who is it?

WHO IS IT?
A poet can create the **voice** of more than one speaker
in a single poem. Do you think the different parts of this
poem are about the same person or two people?

TOOLBOX TIP

16

Poor

I heard of poor.
It means hungry, no food,
No shoes, no place to live.
Nothing good.

It means winter nights
And being cold.
It is lonely, alone,
Feeling old.

Poor is a tired face.
Poor is thin.
Poor is standing outside
Looking in.

—Myra Cohn Livingston

Tough times

TOUGH TIMES

TOOLBOX TIP The United States has problems just like other countries have. Not everyone has enough money for their basic needs of food, shelter, and clothing. Poetry can be an easier way to talk about something tough like poverty.

Commitment in a City

On the street we two pass.
I do not know you.
I do not see
if you are—
fat/thin,
dark/fair,
young/old.

If we should pass again
within the hour,
I would not know it.
Yet—
I am committed to
love you.

You are part of my city,
my universe, my being.
If you were not here
to pass me by,
a piece would be missing
from my jigsaw-puzzle day.

—Margaret Tsuda

TOOLBOX TIP

DIFFERENT POINTS OF VIEW

Both of these poems describe what it is like being in a city. Poets often look at the same thing in different ways. Do both speakers in these poems like the city, or do they see it differently?

City Blockades

I feel so small
standing beneath the tall
buildings that wall
me and the pigeons in
from the light of the
sky.

—Lee Bennett Hopkins

Brooklyn Bridge *(Jump Rope Rhyme)*

Brooklyn Bridge, Brooklyn Bridge,
I walked to the middle, jumped over the
edge,

The water was greasy, the water was
brown

Like cold chop suey in Chinatown,
And I gobbled it up as I sank down,—
Down—
Down—
Down—
Down—

Brooklyn Bridge, Brooklyn Bridge,
I walked to the middle, looked over the
edge.

But I didn't jump off, what I said's
not true—
I just made it up so I could scare you;
Watch me jump!
Watch me jump!
Watch me jump!
BOO!

—William Jay Smith

Repeat the beat

TOOLBOX TIP

REPEAT THE BEAT

If you want to create a **rhythm,** you can repeat things and use different rhymes. You can feel the rhythm, or beat, of a poem just like a tempo in music. This poem has such a good beat that you can jump rope to it.

Time to Play

Mama says to play outside.
Wish I had a bike to ride.
I'll fly to the moon instead.
Steer the rocket in my head.
I'll pretend to find a star
no one else has seen so far.
Then I'll name it after me—
    Africa Lawanda Lee!
But for now I'll grab some chalk,
play hopscotch out on the walk.

—Nikki Grimes

More beats for your feet

TOOLBOX TIP

MORE BEATS FOR YOUR FEET

The speaker in this poem has a great imagination—and a great beat. You can measure this rhythm with **meter.** Just count the beats in each line— there are always seven. Could you jump rope to this poem, too?

After the Picnic

On the Fourth of July, Billy Blake
Gorged on wieners, and pickles, and cake,
   And, then, in the night
   He called out in fright,
"How the Fourth of July makes me ache!"

—Lee Blair

TOOLBOX TIP

A LITTLE TRICK CALLED "LIMERICK"

The beat in this poem probably seems familiar. It's a **limerick.** The first two lines rhyme with the last line and all have the same number of beats. The third and fourth lines rhyme with each other and have the same number of beats. What a neat trick!

Fourth of July Night

Pin wheels whirling round
Spit sparks upon the ground,
And rockets shoot up high
And blossom in the sky—
Blue and yellow, green and red
Flowers falling on my head,
And I don't ever have to go
To bed, to bed, to bed!

—Dorothy Aldis

Sounds that seem the same

TOOLBOX TIP

SOUNDS THAT SEEM THE SAME

Words can become musical without rhyming. A poet might use **alliteration** to do this. "Wheels whirling," "spit sparks," and "flowers falling" are examples. The sounds "wh," "sp," and "f" repeat in them. Repeating consonants like these or vowels creates alliteration.

Our Flag

How bright our flag
against the sky
atop its flagpole
straight and high!

How bright the red,
the white, the blue,
with what they stand for
shining through,

More meaningful
as years go by . . .
how bright, how bright,
the flag we fly.

—Aileen Fisher

TOOLBOX TIP

HIGH-FLYING RHYMES

The flag is an important symbol of freedom to many Americans. This poet uses several pairs of rhymes to express her respect for the flag. Which lines rhyme?

The Star-Spangled Banner

Oh say, can you see, by the dawn's early light,
    What so proudly we hailed at the twilight's last gleaming—
Whose broad stripes and bright stars, through the perilous fight,
    O'er the ramparts we watched were so gallantly streaming!
And the rocket's red glare, the bombs bursting in air,
Gave proof through the night that our flag was still there;
Oh! say, does that star-spangled banner yet wave
O'er the land of the free, and the home of the brave?

—Francis Scott Key

TOOLBOX TIP

A SONG, OR A POEM?

Sometimes, people like a poem so much that they put it to music.
Then a poem becomes part of a song and is known as lyrics. The
Star-Spangled Banner started out as a poem. Can you sing it?

Collect Your Tools

Poets use a lot of tools to build their poems. What poetry tools have you learned about in this book? When you find the answers to the questions on these pages, you're learning to work just like a poet. (Hint: Need help with a word you don't understand? Look in The Poet's Toolbox Glossary on page 28.)

1. When words end in the same sound, they **rhyme,** such as the poem "The Pioneer" on page 8. Find other poems that have rhyming lines. Do the rhymes always appear in the same pattern?

2. Carl Sandburg repeats the phrase "the buffaloes are gone" a lot in his poem (page 10). Are there other poems in this book that use the tool of **repetition?**

3. On page 23, Dorothy Aldis uses **alliteration** when she repeats sounds like "wh" and "sp." Can you find other places where consonant or vowel sounds are repeated in words close to each other?

4. Details like "front porch," "sorrow songs," "dewy night," and "banks of a mighty river" help create the **imagery** in "Aunt Sue's Stories" on pages 14 and 15. Did another poem have a lot of details that helped create a picture for you?

5. The poem "steam engines" (page 11) is a **free verse** poem—it doesn't use rhyming words or stick to set patterns. Find another free verse poem in this book.

Congratulations! Now you know a whole lot more about the tools poets use, and you're probably able to use some of these tools yourself. You've seen lots of examples. Now go to the next page, and get out your pencil and paper. It's time to build your own poems!

It's time to go to work and use some of the poetry tools you've learned about. Here's an activity that will help you start writing some of your own poems.

Post Your Poetry on the World Wide Web

Publish your own poems on the Web!

1. Get a notebook, something small that you can carry all the time. It can be a plain notebook, nothing fancy.

2. Once a day, sit down to write in your journal. You might find it easy to remember to write in your journal if you decide to do it at the same time each day.

3. What goes in your journal? Anything! Write down whatever grabbed your attention that day. For instance, these are some of the things you can write in your journal: people, places, things, dreams, even your senses—what you've smelled, heard, seen, or touched.

4. Having trouble getting started? The first few days just write down three journal entries. Keep it simple—don't write too much about each thing, just a couple of sentences. After a few days, write four entries a day. Keep adding more as the days pass.

5. Next, become a poet. After a week of keeping a journal, read back over what you've written. Choose one entry that you really like, an entry that shows you something you can really see clearly. Then look at the poet's tools you practiced on the previous page. Try using some of those tools—like alliteration, rhyming, rhythm, or repetition—to turn your journal entries into poems.

6. Finally, post your poetry to the Web. Use some of the sites from FactHound on page 31 to find places that accept student poetry. Follow the site's instructions, and your poem might make it onto a poetry page!

Go to Work

The Poet's Toolbox Glossary can help you understand poetry tools used in this book and others in this series. Words in **color** are tools found in this book. Words in **black** are other poetry tools that will also be helpful as you work on your own poetry.

Acrostic poems use the first letters of each line to spell out a word or name.

Alliteration (ah-LIT-er-A-shun) is a tool that helps with sounds. It repeats consonant sounds or vowel sounds that are the same, like the "m" in "marvelous malted milk" or the "o" sound in "Go home, Joe."

Comparing and contrasting helps you to see what is the same or different about two or more ideas, objects, people, places, or anything. For example, a poet might compare an old shoe to a new shoe by listing the way the two shoes smell (stinky or fresh), look (dirty or clean), and feel (comfortable or stiff).

Concrete poems look like something you can touch. The way words and lines are arranged on the page is just as important as what they mean. A poem about the sun might be round like the sun, or a poem about a swing might look like the words are swinging.

Couplets are pairs of rhyming lines that usually have the same number of beats. Couplets make their own point, create a separate image, or summarize the idea of a poem.

Free verse poetry is poetry that doesn't have to rhyme or stay in stanzas, or even lines. Don't let the word "free" trick you, though. The poet might use other tools to keep the poem tied together, like repeating the same sounds or words.

Haiku usually has 17 syllables (or beats) in three lines—five syllables in the first and last lines and seven in the middle. A haiku is a short poem, usually about nature and the seasons.

28

Imagery is what you picture in your mind when you read a poem. Details like colors, sounds, sizes, shapes, comparisons, smells, and flavors all help create imagery.

Limericks are humorous poems with five lines. The last words of the first, second, and fifth lines rhyme, as do the last words of the shorter third and fourth lines. The shorter lines have two stressed beats, and the longer lines have three stressed beats.

Metaphors show how two different things are similar by calling one thing something else, such as if you call clouds "balls of cotton."

Meter measures the number of syllables, or beats, in each line of a poem. If you can count the beats, you can determine the meter. For example, some types of poems always have 10 beats per line. Others have 12.

Onomatopoeia (ON-o-MA-tow-PEE-ya) is another cool word tool that poets use. This is when the word suggests the sound or action it means, like "buzz," "hiss," and "boom."

Patterns are several things that are repeated in the same way several times. Many poems create a pattern by repeating rhyming words at the end of each line.

Personification gives human characteristics, or traits, to something that isn't human. It makes an object or animal seem human or come to life.

Repetition is what happens when poets repeat certain words, phrases, or sounds. Repetition can help create patterns. It can also help make or emphasize a point.

Rhymes are words that end in the same sound. For example, "clock" rhymes with "dock." Rhyming sounds don't have to be spelled the same way. "Pest" rhymes with "dressed."

Rhythm is the beat you can feel in poetry, like a tempo in music. Syllables, or beats, help create rhythm. Rhymes can create rhythm, too. You can measure rhythm through meter.

Similes are comparisons using "as" or "like." When you use a simile, you are saying that one thing is similar to another. Similes can help you create personification. They are also a lot like metaphors.

Stanzas are like paragraphs for poetry. They are groups of lines that sit together and are usually separated by a blank line. Sometimes a poet begins a new thought in a new stanza.

Structure is how a poem was built. A poet can build a poem using lines and stanzas.

Synonyms are words that mean almost the same thing.

Translated means that the poem was originally written in a different language.

Voice is the speaker in a poem. It can be one person, or a bunch of different people. It can be animals, objects, or even the poet.

AT THE LIBRARY

Alarcón, Francisco X. Illustrated by Maya Christina Gonzalez. *From the Bellybutton of the Moon and Other Summer Poems.* San Francisco: Children's Book Press, 1998.

Hughes, Langston. Illustrated by Brian Pinkney. *The Dream Keeper and Other Poems.* New York: Knopf, 1994.

Kennedy, X.J. Illustrated by Joy Allen. *Exploding Gravy: Poems to Make You Laugh.* Boston: Little, Brown, 2002.

Lansky, Bruce. Illustrated by Stephen Carpenter. *If Pigs Could Fly—And Other Deep Thoughts: A Collection of Funny Poems.* Minnetonka, Minn.: Meadowbrook Press, 2000.

Shapiro, Karen Jo. Illustrated by Matt Faulkner. *Because I Could Not Stop My Bike, and Other Poems.* Watertown, Mass.: Whispering Coyote, 2003.

Silverstein, Shel. *Falling Up: Poems and Drawings.* New York: HarperCollins, 1996.

Wong, Janet S. *A Suitcase of Seaweed, and Other Poems.* New York: Margaret K. McElderry Books, 1996.

ON THE ROAD

Riley Museum

528 Lockerbie St.

Indianapolis, IN 46202

317/631-5885

To visit the historical Victorian home of poet

James Whitcomb Riley

WEB SITES

For more information on **poetry,** use FactHound
to track down Web sites related to this book.

1. Go to *www.compasspointbooks.com/facthound*

2. Type in this book ID: **0756505631**

3. Click on the FETCH IT button.

Your trusty FactHound will fetch the best Web sites for you!

ABOUT THE AUTHOR

Patricia M. Stockland has a Bachelor of Arts degree in English from South Dakota State University. She lives in Minnesota and is currently completing her Master of Arts thesis in literature from Minnesota State University, Mankato. She has taught composition and enjoys both writing and helping others write. Patricia is an editor and author of children's nonfiction books.

ABOUT THE ILLUSTRATOR

Sara Rojo Pérez was born in Madrid and now lives in Cádiz on the southern coast of Spain. For many years she worked as the creative director of an animation studio, creating both films and advertisements. Sara works in many different media—from paint in oils or acrylics to computer illustration to sculptures and tapestries. In addition to her artwork, Sara enjoys horseback riding and reading fantasy and mystery novels.

32

INDEX